PRACTICE 1   PRACTICE 2

MATCH NOTES

REFLECTION   IMPROVEMENTS

PRACTICE 1　　　　PRACTICE 2

MATCH NOTES

REFLECTION　　　　IMPROVEMENTS

PRACTICE 1 PRACTICE 2

MATCH NOTES

REFLECTION IMPROVEMENTS

PRACTICE 1   PRACTICE 2

MATCH NOTES

REFLECTION   IMPROVEMENTS

PRACTICE 1　　　PRACTICE 2

MATCH NOTES

REFLECTION　　　IMPROVEMENTS

PRACTICE 1　　　　PRACTICE 2

MATCH NOTES

REFLECTION　　　IMPROVEMENTS

PRACTICE 1   PRACTICE 2

MATCH NOTES

REFLECTION   IMPROVEMENTS

PRACTICE 1   PRACTICE 2

MATCH NOTES

REFLECTION   IMPROVEMENTS

PRACTICE 1   PRACTICE 2

MATCH NOTES

REFLECTION   IMPROVEMENTS

PRACTICE 1   PRACTICE 2

MATCH NOTES

REFLECTION   IMPROVEMENTS

PRACTICE 1　　　　　PRACTICE 2

MATCH NOTES

REFLECTION　　　　IMPROVEMENTS

PRACTICE 1　　　　　PRACTICE 2

MATCH NOTES

REFLECTION　　　　　IMPROVEMENTS

PRACTICE 1   PRACTICE 2

MATCH NOTES

REFLECTION   IMPROVEMENTS

PRACTICE 1   PRACTICE 2

MATCH NOTES

REFLECTION   IMPROVEMENTS

PRACTICE 1

PRACTICE 2

MATCH NOTES

REFLECTION

IMPROVEMENTS

PRACTICE 1   PRACTICE 2

MATCH NOTES

REFLECTION   IMPROVEMENTS

PRACTICE 1
PRACTICE 2

MATCH NOTES

REFLECTION
IMPROVEMENTS

PRACTICE 1   PRACTICE 2

MATCH NOTES

REFLECTION   IMPROVEMENTS

PRACTICE 1　　　PRACTICE 2

MATCH NOTES

REFLECTION　　IMPROVEMENTS

PRACTICE 1   PRACTICE 2

MATCH NOTES

REFLECTION   IMPROVEMENTS

PRACTICE 1   PRACTICE 2

MATCH NOTES

REFLECTION   IMPROVEMENTS

PRACTICE 1   PRACTICE 2

MATCH NOTES

REFLECTION   IMPROVEMENTS

PRACTICE 1   PRACTICE 2

MATCH NOTES

REFLECTION   IMPROVEMENTS

PRACTICE 1   PRACTICE 2

MATCH NOTES

REFLECTION   IMPROVEMENTS

PRACTICE 1　　PRACTICE 2

MATCH NOTES

REFLECTION　　IMPROVEMENTS

PRACTICE 1　　　PRACTICE 2

MATCH NOTES

REFLECTION　　IMPROVEMENTS

PRACTICE 1   PRACTICE 2

MATCH NOTES

REFLECTION   IMPROVEMENTS

PRACTICE 1   PRACTICE 2

MATCH NOTES

REFLECTION   IMPROVEMENTS

PRACTICE 1   PRACTICE 2

MATCH NOTES

REFLECTION   IMPROVEMENTS

PRACTICE 1   PRACTICE 2

MATCH NOTES

REFLECTION   IMPROVEMENTS

PRACTICE 1   PRACTICE 2

MATCH NOTES

REFLECTION   IMPROVEMENTS

PRACTICE 1　　　　PRACTICE 2

MATCH NOTES

REFLECTION　　　　IMPROVEMENTS

PRACTICE 1   PRACTICE 2

MATCH NOTES

REFLECTION   IMPROVEMENTS

PRACTICE 1   PRACTICE 2

MATCH NOTES

REFLECTION   IMPROVEMENTS

PRACTICE 1   PRACTICE 2

MATCH NOTES

REFLECTION   IMPROVEMENTS

PRACTICE 1   PRACTICE 2

MATCH NOTES

REFLECTION   IMPROVEMENTS

PRACTICE 1   PRACTICE 2

MATCH NOTES

REFLECTION   IMPROVEMENTS

PRACTICE 1   PRACTICE 2

MATCH NOTES

REFLECTION   IMPROVEMENTS

PRACTICE 1   PRACTICE 2

MATCH NOTES

REFLECTION   IMPROVEMENTS

PRACTICE 1   PRACTICE 2

MATCH NOTES

REFLECTION   IMPROVEMENTS

PRACTICE 1　　　　PRACTICE 2

MATCH NOTES

REFLECTION　　　IMPROVEMENTS

PRACTICE 1　　　PRACTICE 2

MATCH NOTES

REFLECTION　　　IMPROVEMENTS

PRACTICE 1　　　PRACTICE 2

MATCH NOTES

REFLECTION　　　IMPROVEMENTS

PRACTICE 1   PRACTICE 2

MATCH NOTES

REFLECTION   IMPROVEMENTS

PRACTICE 1   PRACTICE 2

MATCH NOTES

REFLECTION   IMPROVEMENTS

PRACTICE 1   PRACTICE 2

MATCH NOTES

REFLECTION   IMPROVEMENTS

PRACTICE 1   PRACTICE 2

MATCH NOTES

REFLECTION   IMPROVEMENTS

PRACTICE 1   PRACTICE 2

MATCH NOTES

REFLECTION   IMPROVEMENTS

PRACTICE 1   PRACTICE 2

MATCH NOTES

REFLECTION   IMPROVEMENTS

PRACTICE 1   PRACTICE 2

MATCH NOTES

REFLECTION   IMPROVEMENTS

PRACTICE 1   PRACTICE 2

MATCH NOTES

REFLECTION   IMPROVEMENTS

PRACTICE 1   PRACTICE 2

MATCH NOTES

REFLECTION   IMPROVEMENTS

PRACTICE 1   PRACTICE 2

MATCH NOTES

REFLECTION   IMPROVEMENTS

PRACTICE 1   PRACTICE 2

MATCH NOTES

REFLECTION   IMPROVEMENTS

PRACTICE 1   PRACTICE 2

MATCH NOTES

REFLECTION   IMPROVEMENTS

PRACTICE 1   PRACTICE 2

MATCH NOTES

REFLECTION   IMPROVEMENTS

PRACTICE 1　　　PRACTICE 2

MATCH NOTES

REFLECTION　　　IMPROVEMENTS

PRACTICE 1   PRACTICE 2

MATCH NOTES

REFLECTION   IMPROVEMENTS

PRACTICE 1　　　　PRACTICE 2

MATCH NOTES

REFLECTION　　　　IMPROVEMENTS

PRACTICE 1   PRACTICE 2

MATCH NOTES

REFLECTION   IMPROVEMENTS

PRACTICE 1   PRACTICE 2

MATCH NOTES

REFLECTION   IMPROVEMENTS

PRACTICE 1   PRACTICE 2

MATCH NOTES

REFLECTION   IMPROVEMENTS

PRACTICE 1

PRACTICE 2

MATCH NOTES

REFLECTION

IMPROVEMENTS

PRACTICE 1   PRACTICE 2

MATCH NOTES

REFLECTION   IMPROVEMENTS

PRACTICE 1 PRACTICE 2

MATCH NOTES

REFLECTION IMPROVEMENTS

PRACTICE 1

PRACTICE 2

MATCH NOTES

REFLECTION

IMPROVEMENTS

PRACTICE 1   PRACTICE 2

MATCH NOTES

REFLECTION   IMPROVEMENTS

PRACTICE 1   PRACTICE 2

MATCH NOTES

REFLECTION   IMPROVEMENTS

PRACTICE 1   PRACTICE 2

MATCH NOTES

REFLECTION   IMPROVEMENTS

PRACTICE 1   PRACTICE 2

MATCH NOTES

REFLECTION   IMPROVEMENTS

PRACTICE 1   PRACTICE 2

MATCH NOTES

REFLECTION   IMPROVEMENTS

PRACTICE 1　　　PRACTICE 2

MATCH NOTES

REFLECTION　　　IMPROVEMENTS

PRACTICE 1　　　　PRACTICE 2

MATCH NOTES

REFLECTION　　　　IMPROVEMENTS

_____
_____
_____

PRACTICE 1   PRACTICE 2

MATCH NOTES

REFLECTION   IMPROVEMENTS

PRACTICE 1   PRACTICE 2

MATCH NOTES

REFLECTION   IMPROVEMENTS

PRACTICE 1 PRACTICE 2

MATCH NOTES

REFLECTION IMPROVEMENTS

PRACTICE 1   PRACTICE 2

MATCH NOTES

REFLECTION   IMPROVEMENTS

PRACTICE 1　　　PRACTICE 2

MATCH NOTES

REFLECTION　　　IMPROVEMENTS

PRACTICE 1   PRACTICE 2

MATCH NOTES

REFLECTION   IMPROVEMENTS

PRACTICE 1   PRACTICE 2

MATCH NOTES

REFLECTION   IMPROVEMENTS

PRACTICE 1   PRACTICE 2

MATCH NOTES

REFLECTION   IMPROVEMENTS

PRACTICE 1   PRACTICE 2

MATCH NOTES

REFLECTION   IMPROVEMENTS

PRACTICE 1   PRACTICE 2

MATCH NOTES

REFLECTION   IMPROVEMENTS

PRACTICE 1

PRACTICE 2

MATCH NOTES

REFLECTION

IMPROVEMENTS

PRACTICE 1　　　PRACTICE 2

MATCH NOTES

REFLECTION　　　IMPROVEMENTS

PRACTICE 1   PRACTICE 2

MATCH NOTES

REFLECTION   IMPROVEMENTS

PRACTICE 1   PRACTICE 2

MATCH NOTES

REFLECTION   IMPROVEMENTS

PRACTICE 1   PRACTICE 2

MATCH NOTES

REFLECTION   IMPROVEMENTS

PRACTICE 1   PRACTICE 2

MATCH NOTES

REFLECTION   IMPROVEMENTS

PRACTICE 1 PRACTICE 2

MATCH NOTES

REFLECTION IMPROVEMENTS

PRACTICE 1   PRACTICE 2

MATCH NOTES

REFLECTION   IMPROVEMENTS

PRACTICE 1 PRACTICE 2

MATCH NOTES

REFLECTION IMPROVEMENTS

PRACTICE 1   PRACTICE 2

MATCH NOTES

REFLECTION   IMPROVEMENTS

PRACTICE 1   PRACTICE 2

MATCH NOTES

REFLECTION   IMPROVEMENTS

PRACTICE 1   PRACTICE 2

MATCH NOTES

REFLECTION   IMPROVEMENTS

PRACTICE 1   PRACTICE 2

MATCH NOTES

REFLECTION   IMPROVEMENTS

PRACTICE 1

PRACTICE 2

MATCH NOTES

REFLECTION

IMPROVEMENTS

PRACTICE 1　　　PRACTICE 2

MATCH NOTES

REFLECTION　　　IMPROVEMENTS

PRACTICE 1　　　　PRACTICE 2

MATCH NOTES

REFLECTION　　　IMPROVEMENTS

PRACTICE 1   PRACTICE 2

MATCH NOTES

REFLECTION   IMPROVEMENTS

Printed in Great Britain
by Amazon